I0488137

Stillpoints

Photo essays by Jonathan Brandstater

Copyright 2014

For Lisa

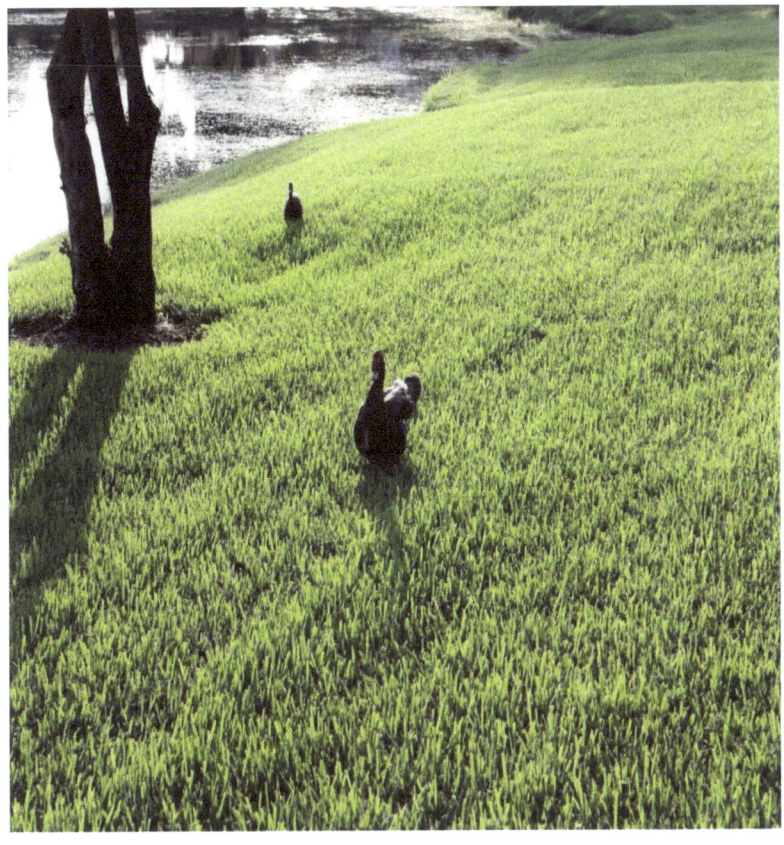

They do not show fear of me but approach at ease and seem to enjoy the attention. It is not often I meet ducks willing to pose as models for portraits.

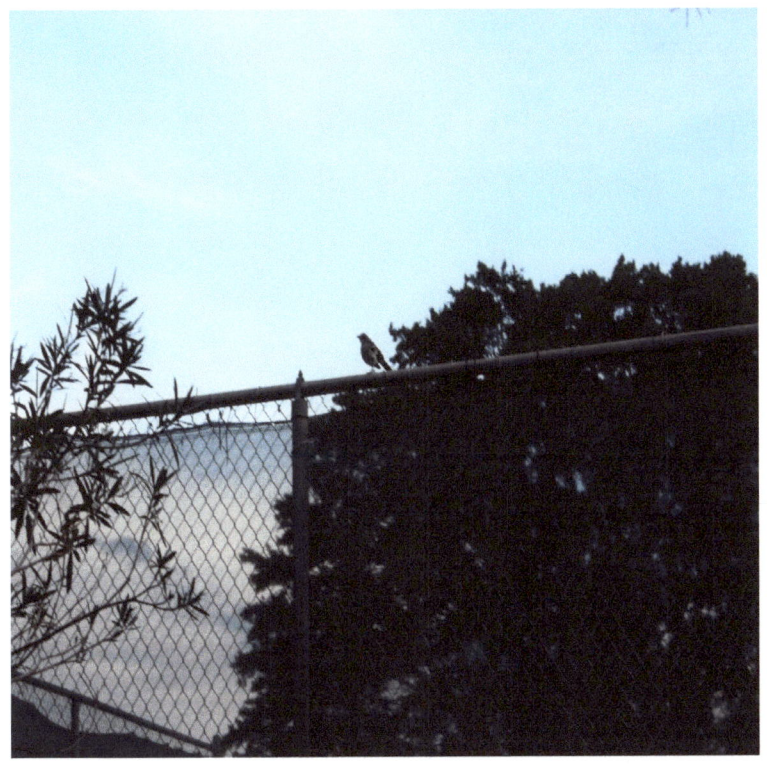

The bird stops to rest on the fence at sunset. Possibly he scans the ground and sky around him/her for predators or potential meals before moving on.

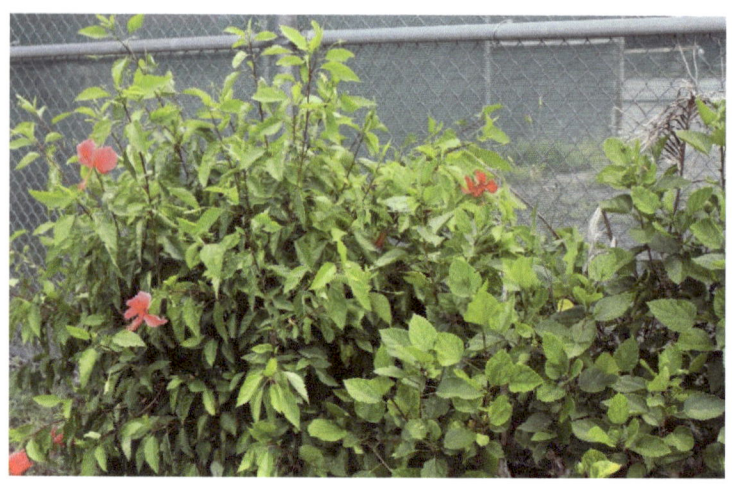

Can you see the butterfly in this picture? Can you see what is hidden in plain sight?

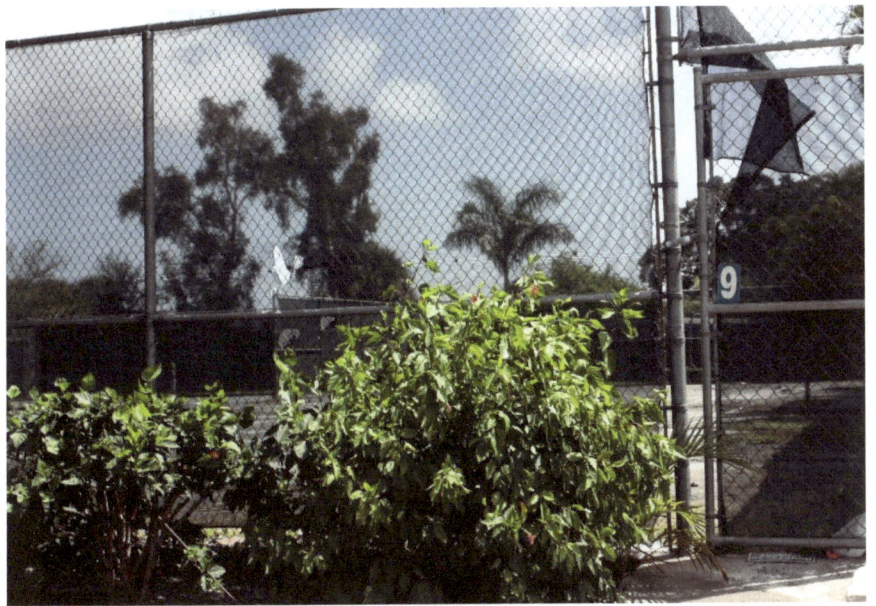

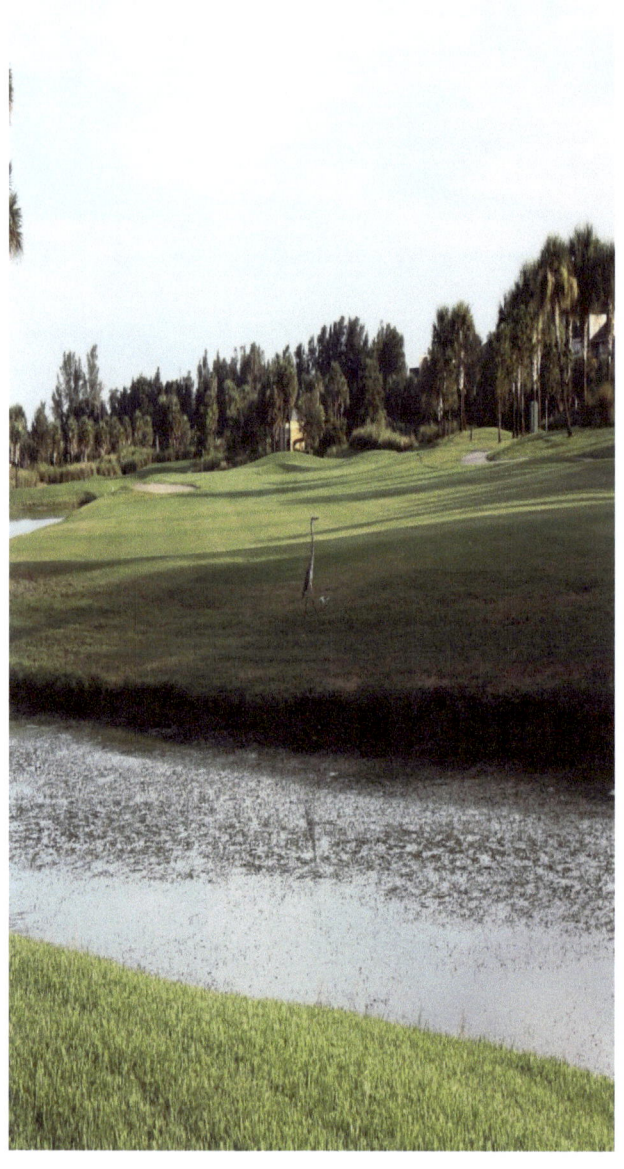

Go with the flow. See where it wants to take you.

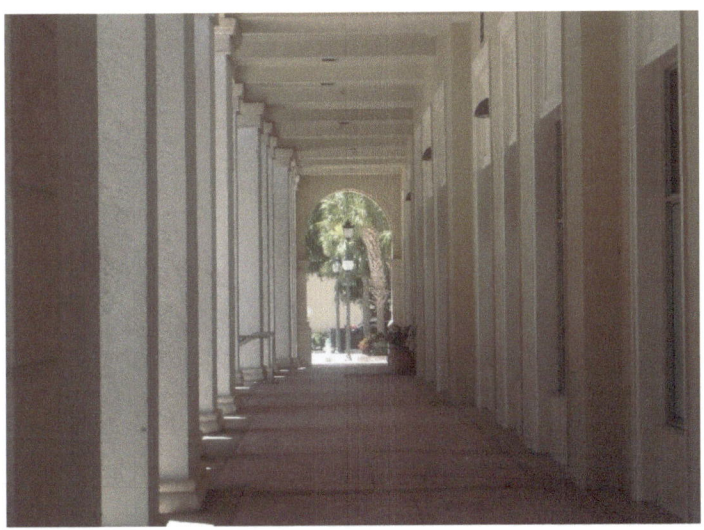

Notice the signs.

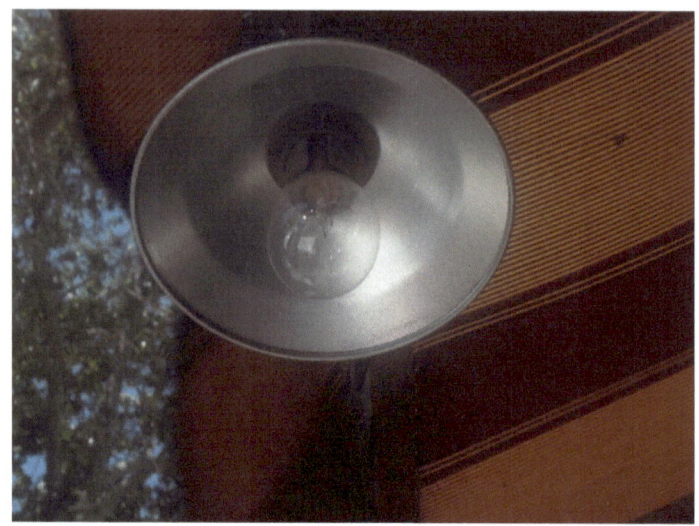

Shine your light.

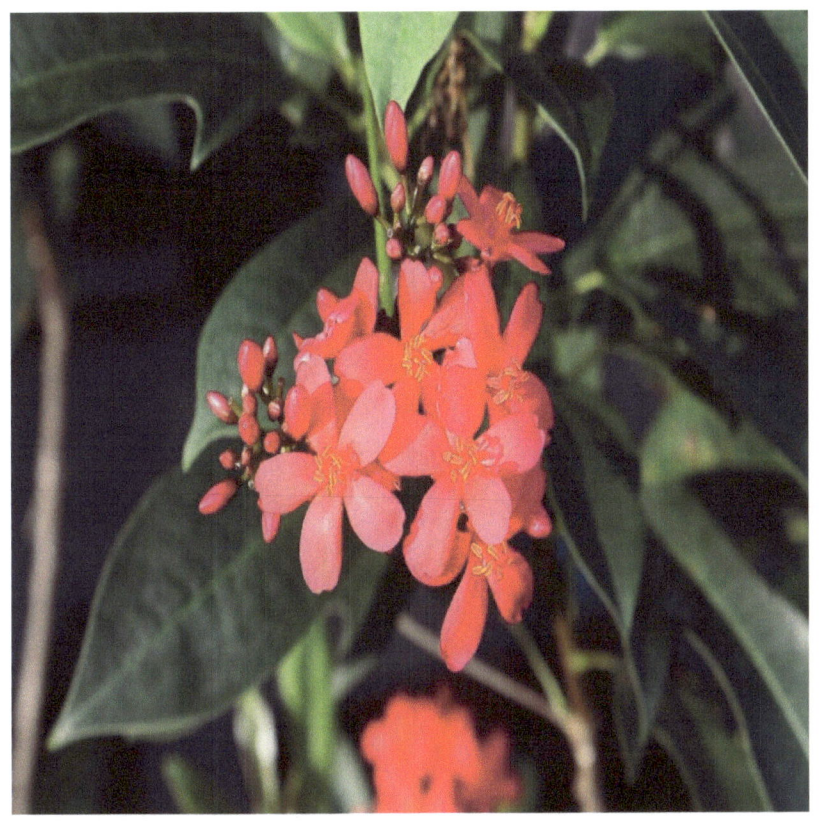

The more you gaze at a flower, the more you notice. The more you notice, the more you appreciate its beauty. There is beauty in simplicity.

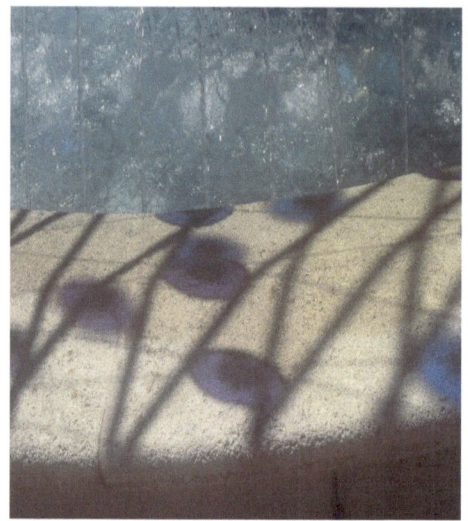

Take time to reflect.

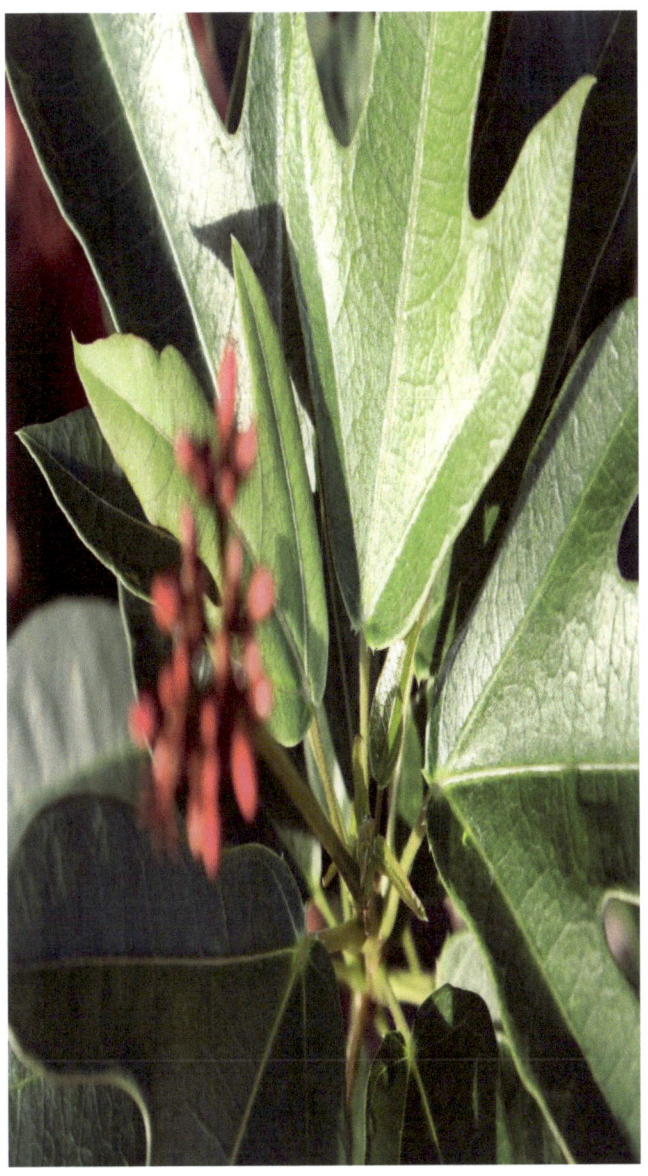

The buds open with no effort. There is much to be learned from their example.

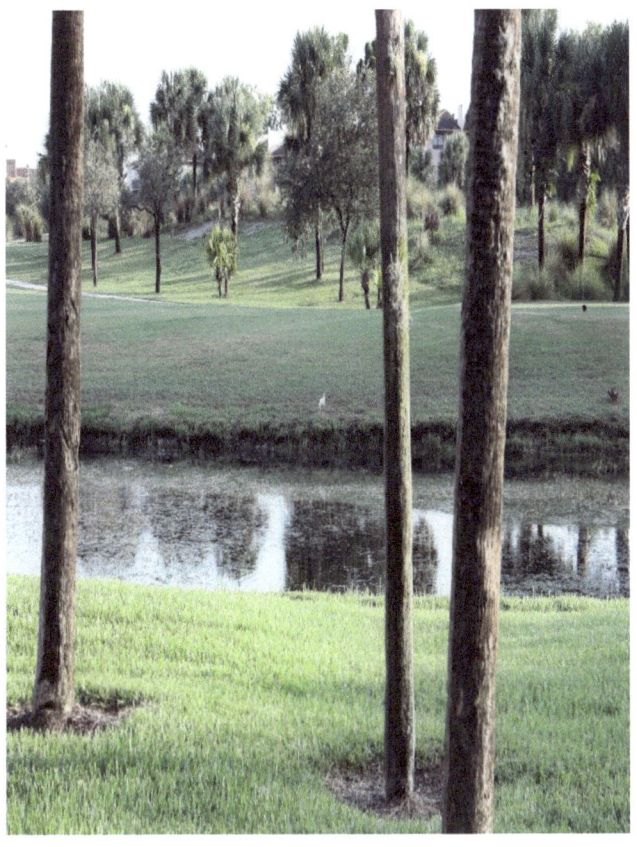

We belong to the Earth. Our roots dig into the ground and our branches reach into the sky. Breathe deeply.

Appreciate the gift of air. It is for everyone and everything.

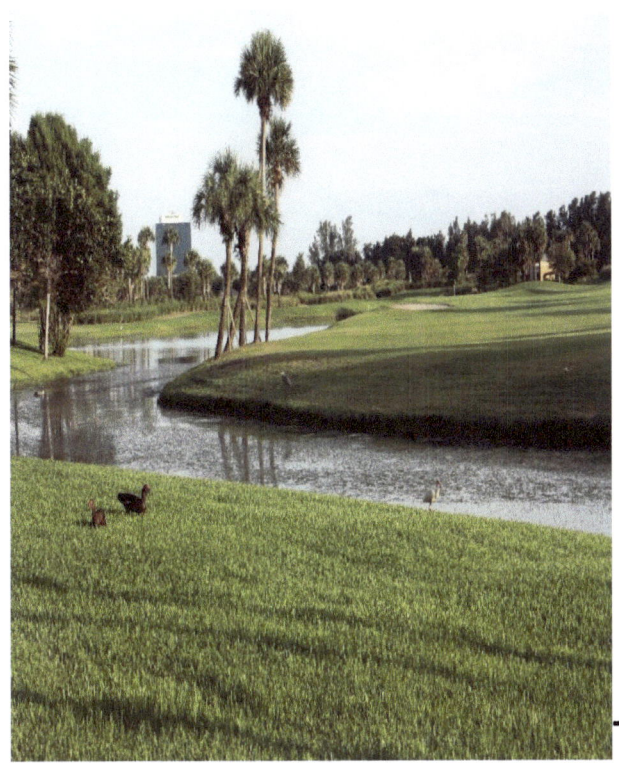

They are at home on the ground, in the water and in the air.

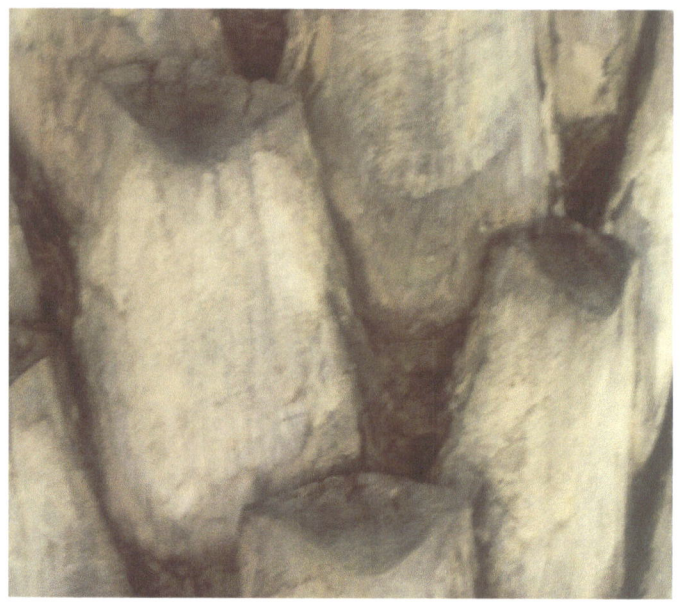

Notice patterns. You will see them in many places, if you take the time to look. There is a sense of order in the universe, regardless of some scientific theories to the contrary.

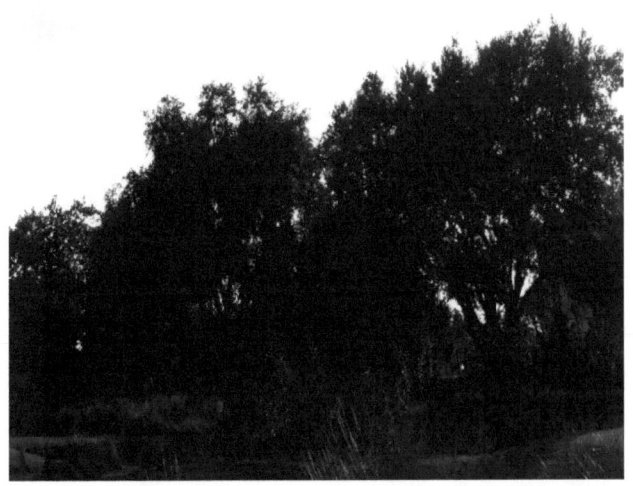

The standing people (trees) provide so much for us: food, shelter, oxygen, beauty, even history.

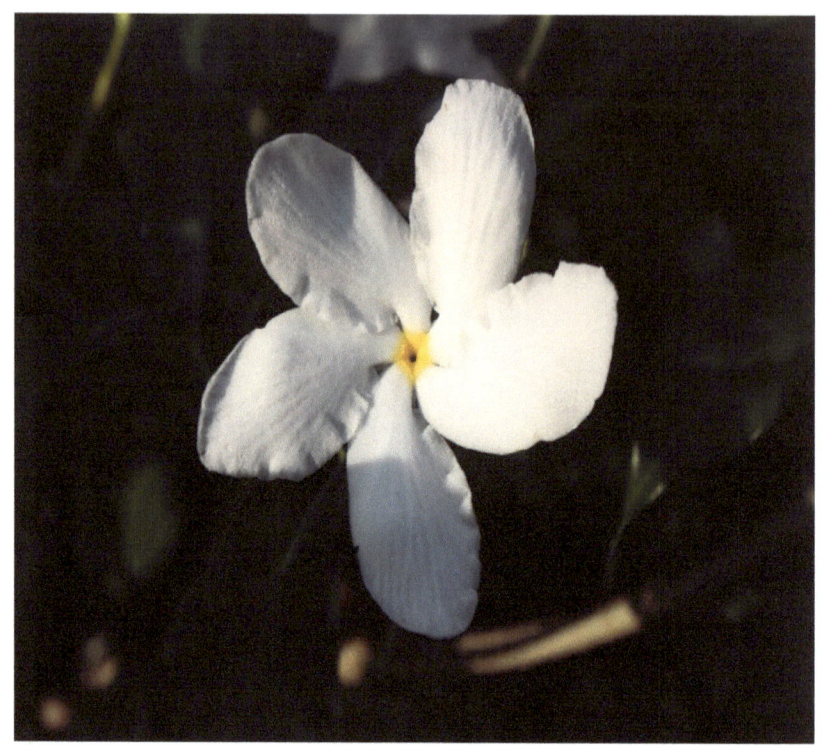

The flower seems to be smiling. Perhaps, in a way, it is. Perhaps the flower is grateful to appear, if only to share its beauty for a brief while.

No two sunsets are alike. No words can adequately describe a sunset. Appreciate the colors, along with the play of light and shadow.

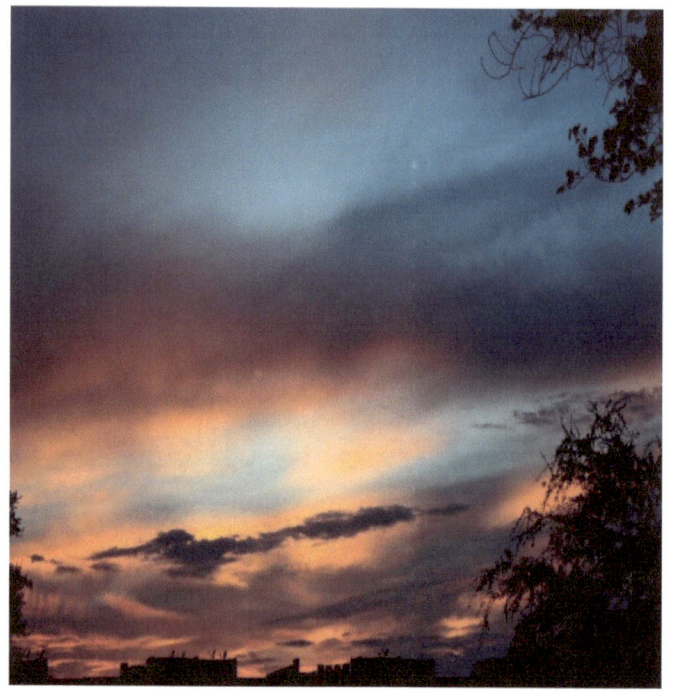

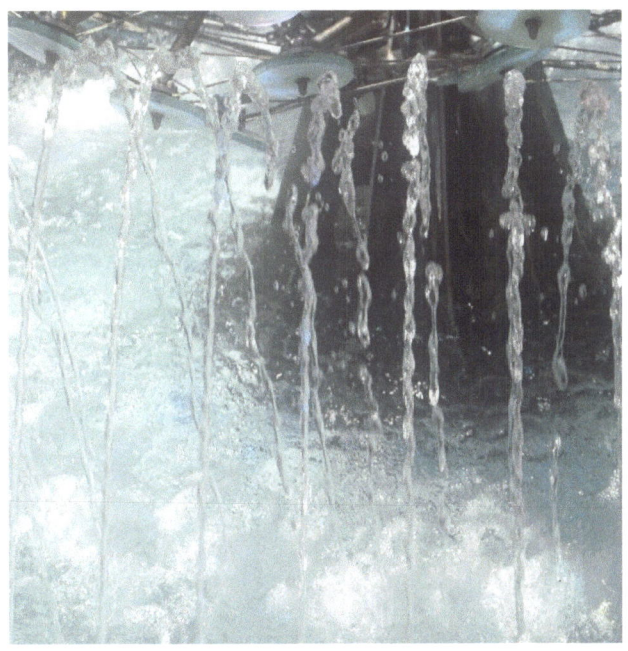

Photo taken with a shutter speed of 1/125 second. Notice the individual droplets of water. How mind boggling it is to consider how many droplets there are in an ocean. Can you imagine a water droplet being itself an ocean?

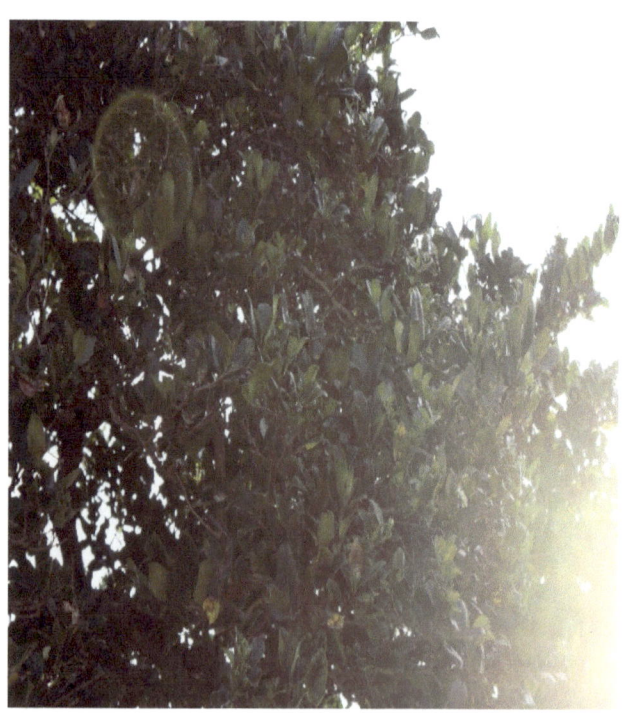

I took this photo not long after watching a DVD about orbs. I doubt the greenish bubble-like object to the upper left is a dust mote, glitch in the camera or trick of the light.

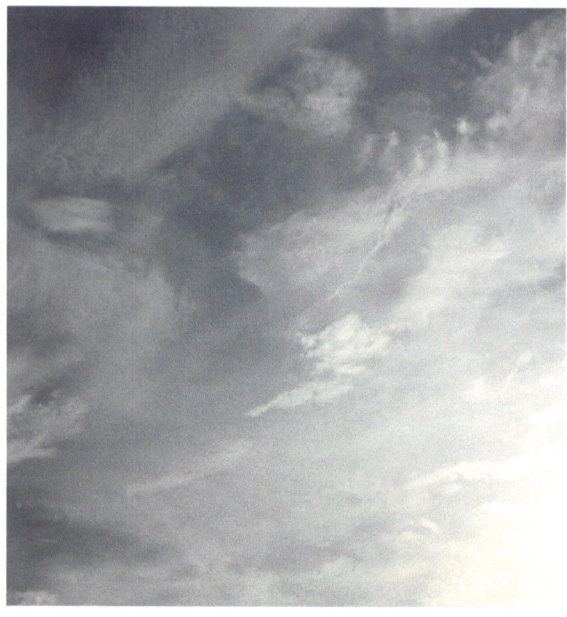

The sky at sunset. Maybe this can be considered a study of form and substance.

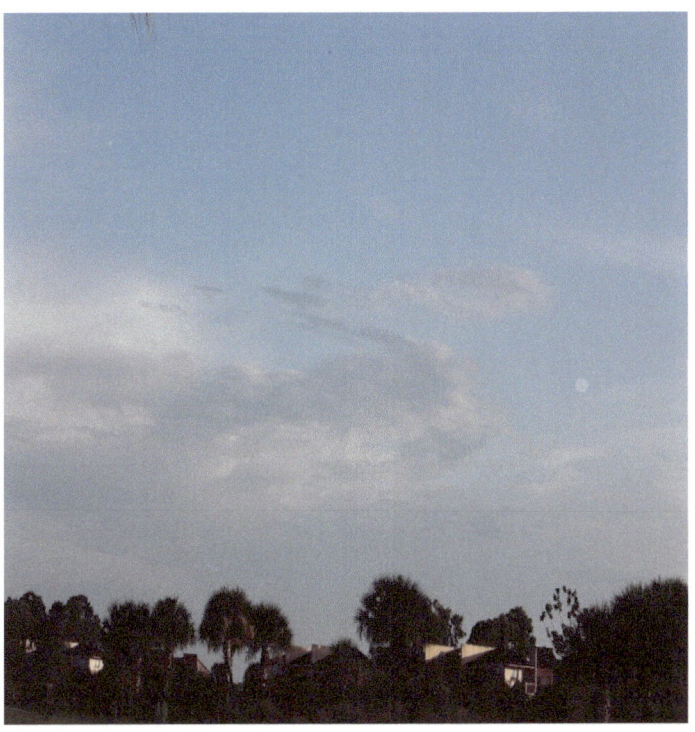

An idyll

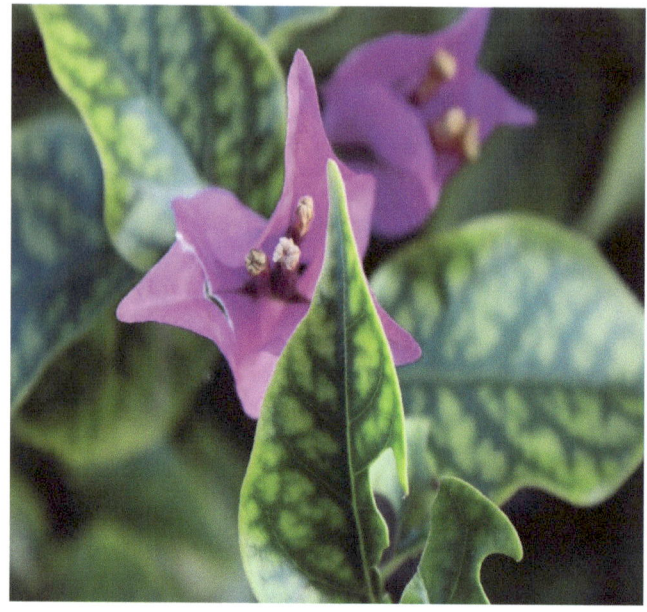

It is all in the details.

A thing of beauty is a joy forever.

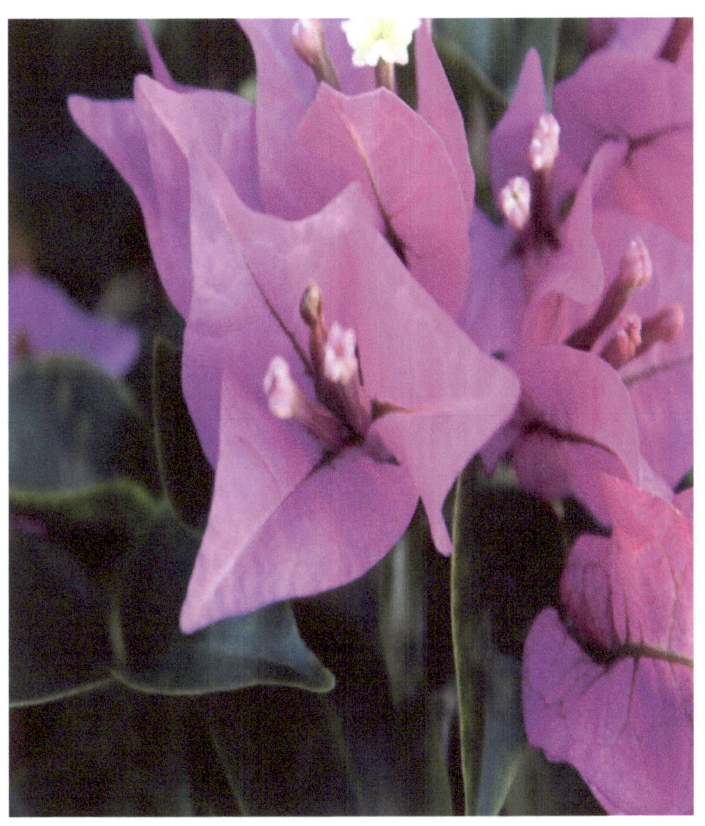

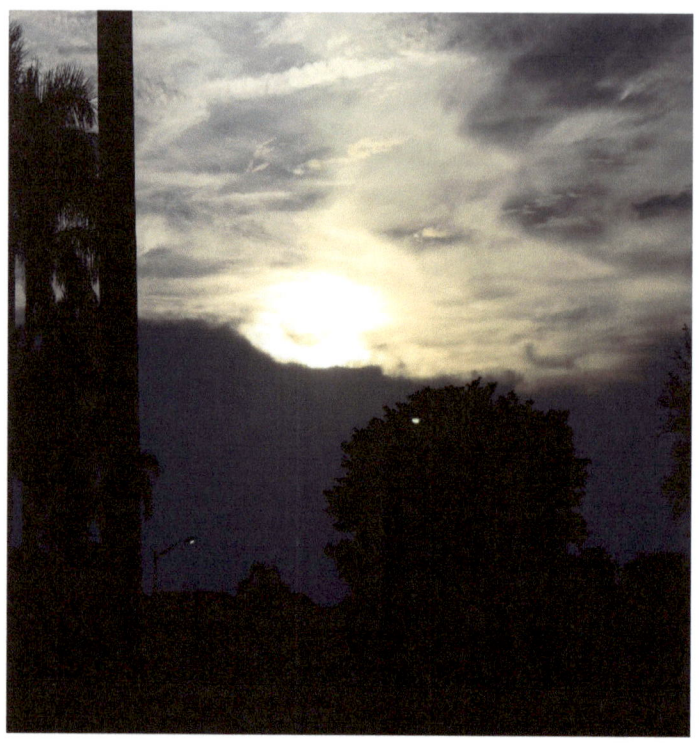

The play of light and shadow at sunset.

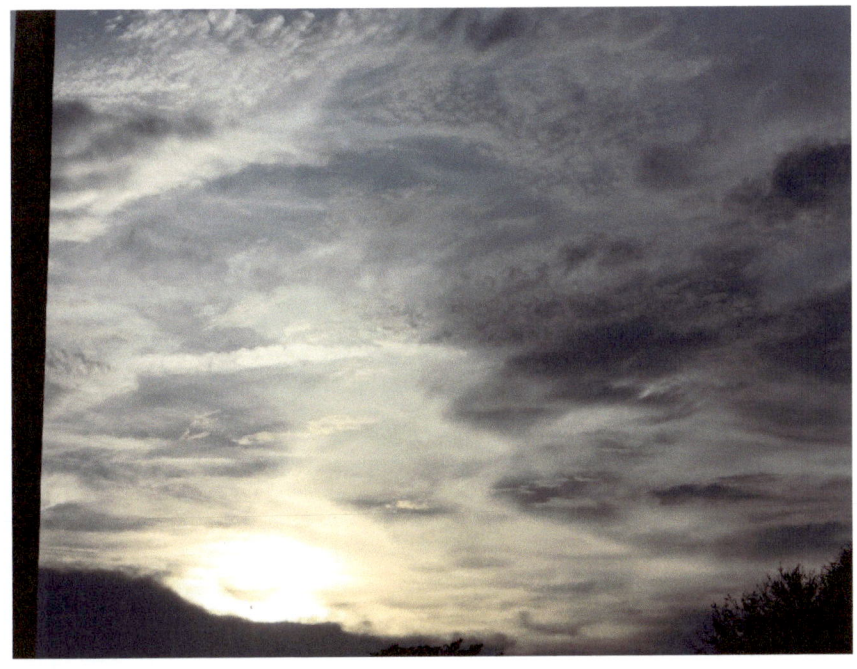

Hues and tints

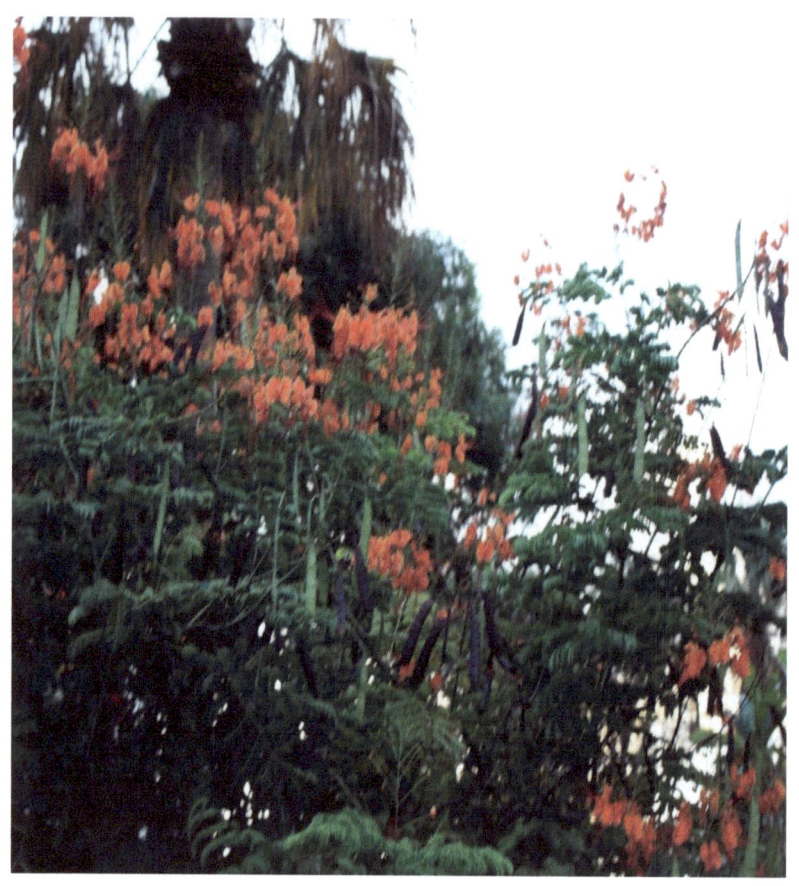

Splashes of color

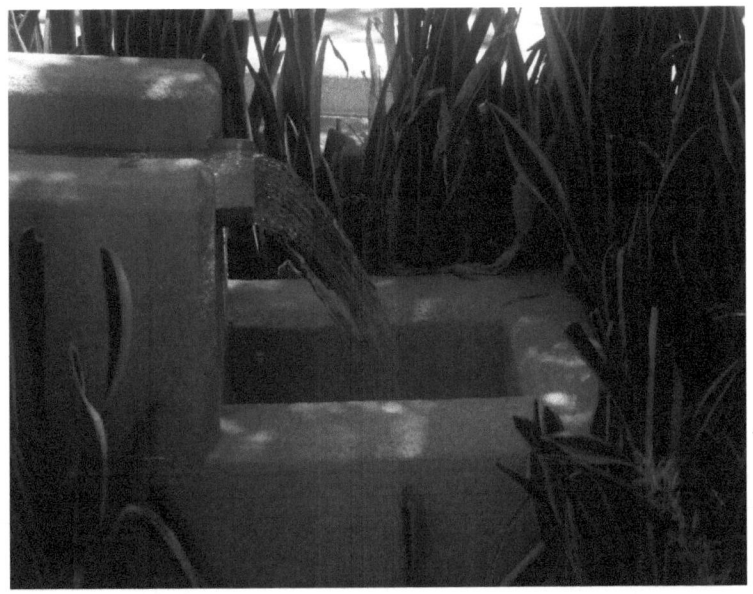

A miniature waterfall

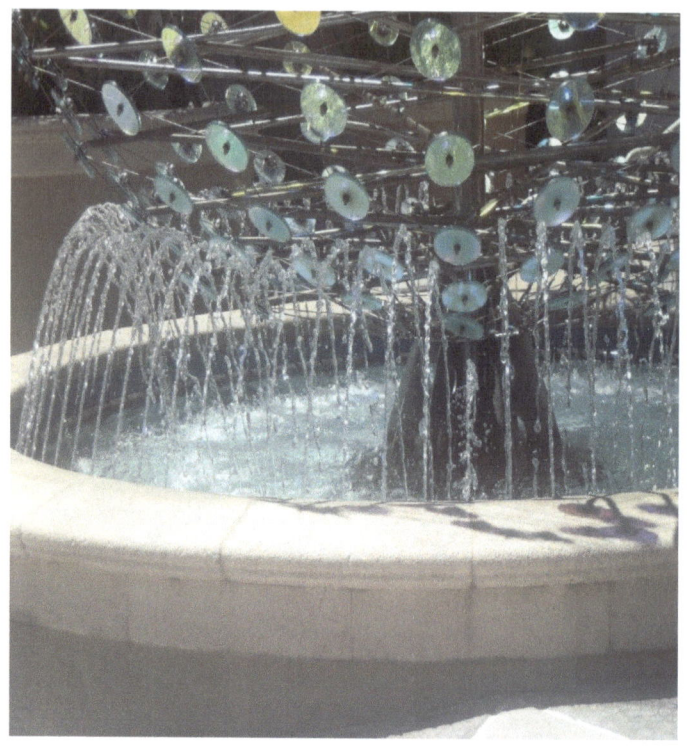

So many rainbows

Imagine the possibilities.

Sometimes the only thing required to solve a problem is a change in perspective.

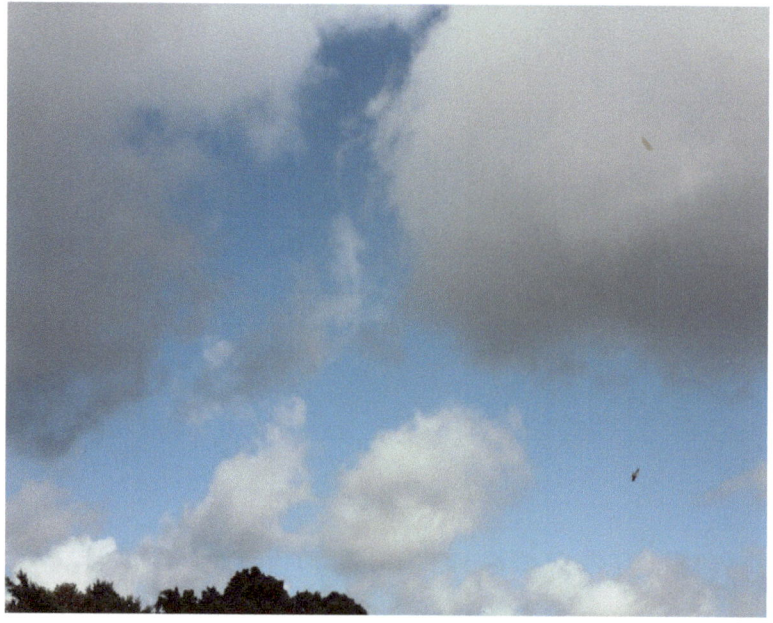

Sometimes big things come in small packages.

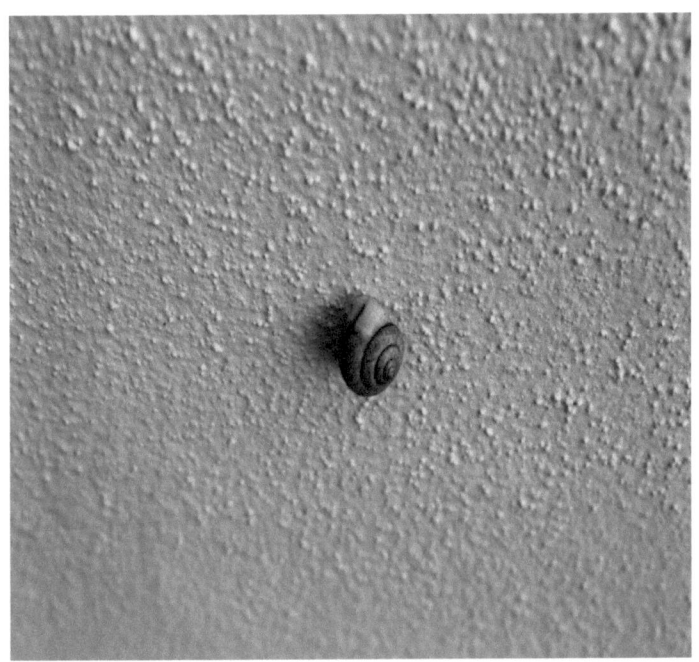

Play in the field of
possibilities.

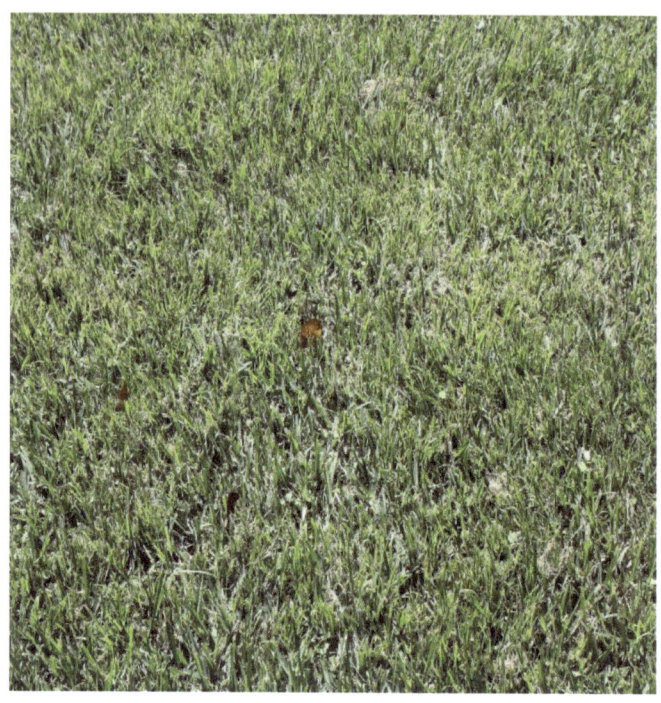

There are no endings, only new beginnings.

www.ingramcontent.com/pod-product-compliance
Lightning Source LLC
Chambersburg PA
CBHW041145180526
45159CB00002BB/739